Is Your Life a **puddle** or an **Ocean?**

Richard Rowe

Insight Publishing
Sevierville, Tennessee

Is Your Life a puddle or an Ocean?

Copyright© 2007 by Richard Rowe

All rights reserved. No portion of this publication may be reproduced, stored in a retrieval system, or transmitted in any form by any means-electronic, mechanical, photocopying, recording, or any other style, except for brief quotations embodied in printed reviews, without the prior written permission of the publisher.

10 9 8 7 6 5 4 3 2

Printed in the United States

ISBN-10: 1-60013-133-6
ISBN-13: 978-1-60013-133-2

Contents

FORWARD vii
ACKNOWLEDGMENTS ix

PART I: WHAT ARE PUDDLES AND OCEANS?

CHAPTER 1
What does the title; Is your life a puddle or an ocean mean?..... 1

CHAPTER 2
The ripple effect 3

CHAPTER 3
There is no such thing as luck... 5

PART II: BECOMING AN OCEAN

CHAPTER 4
The Golden Rule – is it new?.. 11

CHAPTER 5
"It's a Wonderful Life" – what did George Bailey find out?...... 19

CHAPTER 6
Who are Oceans – past, present, positive and negative........... 23

PART III: BEING AN OCEAN AT WORK, HOME, COMMUNITY

CHAPTER 7
Responsibility – who me?... 29

CHAPTER 8
Make a Choice 33

CHAPTER 9
The tenants of becoming an ocean 35

Foreword

I urge you wholeheartedly to hook into the concept of the vast ripple you can create. The power of "one" can be the most powerful force in the world. It is being shared in these pages with the hope that you will rediscover the true essence of how interconnected we are. These pages do not preach, but offer instead a way of approaching the journey of life that will not only benefit everyone with whom you come in contact, but also empower you with goodness which remains the greatest force in the world.

—Loretta Swit

Acknowledgements

To my mother and grandfather – you helped me become what I am – I'm proud to be your son and grandson.

To my wife, Barbara – you saw me as a diamond in the rough and are the star I guild my life's course by.

To my children, Savanna and Garrett – you are what I want to be, my <u>hero's</u> – I'm proud to be your father!

To the Chief's Mess of the United States Navy – you are the backbone of the Navy.

BTC C. O. Bowers
YNCS Phil Heuertz

Thank you for going before me – I have the <u>watch</u>!

Part I

What are puddles and oceans?

"Help your brother's boat across and your own will reach the shore."

—Proverb-Hindu

Chapter 1

What does the title; Is your life a puddle or an ocean mean?

On the first day of existence, we are perfect, and the book of our lives is new and unwritten. We start our journey; our young minds are like sponges absorbing every image and idea. For the first eight years, we are in the imprinting stage. We start to create/discriminate prejudices about things we encounter. Absorbing positive and negative events that create the product, that is, the end result – **ourselves**.

To first understand the concept of influence, look at how one may see a puddle versus an ocean. A puddle is a <u>small</u> pool of water, usually a few inches in depth and several inches or several feet at it's greatest dimension. Puddles are small, with a limited depth – there are limitations of influence on it's surroundings.

An ocean is a vast body of water that covers almost three quarters (71%) of the surface of the Earth. It is apparently <u>limitless</u> in quantity or volume. Oceans have a greater possibility of positive or negative influence of it's surroundings.

From the beginning, we are directly and indirectly influenced by the actions of others, whether as an active or inactive participant. Now place ourselves in the thought of influence. Consider the ability to indirectly control or affect the actions of other people. The meaning of influence therefore depends on who or what is being affected, and to what extent. We can start to see the idea of our lives as puddles or oceans by seeing and feeling our influences on people around us during our daily interactions.

What and how do we influence others? One very important thought – nothing we discuss in this book is <u>new</u>, we have had these concepts since birth but through experience started to confuse the truth (living life from our hearts, and treating people with respect).

A life as a puddle would have *minimum* influence on those around them; this person is possibly concerned with their own profit or gain in life; while the life of an ocean would have *limitless* effects on those around them like waves on a vast sea.

| puddle – minimal |
| ocean – limitless |

"You must be the change you wish to see in the world."
—Mohandas Gandhi

Chapter 2

The ripple effect…

Having a foundational understanding of puddles, oceans and influence is like the foundation of a home – strength of the structure depends on the solid construction of the foundation. This truth is transferable to our lives, (nothing happens by accident) through understanding why things happen we can start to make them happen on purpose.

Go back to the influence idea from chapter one, let us shift our thoughts to it being like a ripple on a pond. Imagine a beautiful pond with its calm, reflective surface. We pick up a smooth stone and toss it into the pond. The reaction that occurs can be defined as Newton's third law: law of reciprocal actions (for every action there is an equal but opposite reaction) we could use mathematical equations to determine how much energy our stone created but it would not help us to see the affect of each ripple.

With this idea, imagine how each one of our actions (verbal or non-verbal) even the lack of actions; ripple out to those around us – how many lives are positively or negatively affected? We can call this the ripple effect of life, and just like that stone we tossed into the pond, we create a ripple around us.

What ripples do we create? Remember that a puddle is a small pool of water – minimal, but an ocean is limitless.

We create the conditions in our lives and must start to identify **cause and effect**. When we blame others for what happens to us then we give them the power to control who we become. Ripples can be as simple as a smile or more complex like helping someone to get a job and the amazing thing is that they will affect thousands of people because the motion continues unless an object (other persons) stop it.

> The Ripple Effect
>
> *"Each choice we make causes a ripple effect in our lives.*
> *When things happen to us, it is the reaction we choose that can create the difference between the sorrows of our past and the joy in our future."*
>
> —Chelle Thompson

"I trust that everything happens for a reason, even when we're not wise enough to see it."

—Oprah Winfrey, O Magazine

Chapter 3

There is no such thing as luck…

During life, people create names to explain what they do not understand. The terms good luck or bad luck are often used when we achieve success or when we fail. When we put ripples into the world, funny things happen – they affect everything around us and are a direct result for success or failure.

Around the 700 AD timeframe, Vikings would name meteorological events because they had no point of reference for why they happened. When they saw lighting in the sky, it confused and scared them so they had to create a reason for the event. Of course, there is more to the story but Odin became a physical presence to understand why lightning happened – he was known as the god of war and death, but also the god of poetry and wisdom. The companion to lightning is thunder, so Thor, the god of thunder, son of Odin was added. We know that lightning is created by static charges during the convection process, but try to explain that to a Norse warrior back in the day.

We have the same issue our Norse friends had in explaining the unknown or the unexplainable based on our experience or knowledge. When something good happens, we call it good luck or bad luck depending on the condition of the outcome. My personal thought is that there is no such thing as luck. Our human condition and situational outcomes occur because of ripples around us, and are subject to positive or negative conditions. Remember from the previous chapter, every action or lack of action creates ripples and they affect everything around us.

> *"I feel that luck is preparation meeting opportunity."*
> —Oprah Winfrey

What happens on that same pond if several stones are dropped at different areas at the same time? We see multiple ripples intersecting, bouncing off each and creating incredible effects, each of them causing changes. Now place each one of our daily actions in the same scenario, everything we do or not do, say or not say affects everyone around us. Place this idea in relationship to the puddle or ocean – we are all connected, not just on a local level but throughout the world, even through generations. Our lives are like a complex tapestry and every thread is a life we encounter, if one is missing then the picture sacrifices.

Everything in life happens for a reason and understanding why it happens empowers us to change outcomes – we could create a ripple in life today and see the final effect ten years from now. Consider how phobias may by created? Think about a person who has arachnophobia

> *"Kind words can be short and easy to speak, but their echoes are truly endless."*
> —Mother Teresa

(fear of spiders); babies are not born with this fear, but this fear could be created by an event. Maybe at the age of five a big brother threw a spider on them, creating a fear of spiders by an event beyond their control which scared them half to death. The spider never bit or hurt the child but the trauma of it being thrown on him possibly set a pattern for the future. The brother created a ripple by throwing the spider on his sibling – cause and effect at its best. We can apply this idea to each of our lives, what if that person next to you at work, or even in the grocery store needs a smile or word of kindness – if you provide it the results could be extraordinary.

If a person in need is not helped, who is to blame? What is the cost of the ripples we project?

Part II

Becoming an Ocean

"You can have everything in life you want if you will just help enough other people get what they want."
—Zig Zigler

Chapter 4

The Golden Rule – is it new?

Understanding our life as a puddle or an ocean, combined with our understanding of the ripple effect we now need to look at how to create the right ripples – we should clarify that what we put out in life can be both positive or negative. During recent talks, the question has been raised – "Is the Golden Rule a recent concept (within the last few hundred years)?" No; we can see evidence of this idea in several different religions and has been talked about by the world's greatest philosophers'. For example:

Bahá'í World Faith:

"Ascribe not to any soul that which thou wouldst not have ascribed to thee, and say not that which thou doest not." "Blessed is he who preferreth his brother before himself." Baha'u'llah

"And if thine eyes be turned towards justice, choose thou for thy neighbor that which thou choosest for thyself." Epistle to the Son of the Wolf

Brahmanism:

"This is the sum of Dharma [duty]: Do naught unto others which would cause you pain if done to you". Mahabharata, 5:1517

Buddhism:

"...a state that is not pleasing or delightful to me, how could I inflict that upon another?" Samyutta NIkaya v. 353

Hurt not others in ways that you yourself would find hurtful." Udana-Varga 5:18

Christianity:

"Therefore all things whatsoever ye would that men should do to you, do ye even so to them: for this is the law and the prophets." Matthew 7:12, King James Version.

"And as ye would that men should do to you, do ye also to them likewise." **Luke 6:31, King James Version.**

"...and don't do what you hate...", Gospel of Thomas 6. The Gospel of Thomas is one of about 40 gospels that were widely accepted among early Christians, but which never made it into the Christian Scriptures (New Testament).

Confucianism:

"Do not do to others what you do not want them to do to you" Analects 15:23

"Tse-kung asked, 'Is there one word that can serve as a principle of conduct for life?' Confucius replied, 'It is the word

'shu' -- reciprocity. Do not impose on others what you yourself do not desire'" Doctrine of the Mean 13.3

"Try your best to treat others as you would wish to be treated yourself, and you will find that this is the shortest way to benevolence." Mencius VII.A.4

Ancient Egyptian:

"Do for one who may do for you, that you may cause him thus to do." The Tale of the Eloquent Peasant, 109 - 110 Translated by R.B. Parkinson. The original dates to 1970 to 1640 BCE and may be the earliest version ever written. [1]

Hinduism:

"This is the sum of duty: do not do to others what would cause pain if done to you." Mahabharata 5:1517

Humanism:

"(5) Humanists acknowledge human interdependence, the need for mutual respect and the kinship of all humanity."

"(11) Humanists affirm that individual and social problems can only be resolved by means of human reason, intelligent effort, critical thinking joined with compassion and a spirit of empathy for all living beings." [2]

"Don't do things you wouldn't want to have done to you, British Humanist Society." [1]

Islam:

"None of you [truly] believes until he wishes for his brother what he wishes for himself." Number 13 of Imam "Al-Nawawi's

Forty Hadiths." [3]

Jainism:

"*Therefore, neither does he [a sage] cause violence to others nor does he make others do so."* Acarangasutra 5.101-2.

"*In happiness and suffering, in joy and grief, we should regard all creatures as we regard our own self.*" Lord Mahavira, 24th Tirthankara

"*A man should wander about treating all creatures as he himself would be treated.*" Sutrakritanga 1.11.33

Judaism:

"*...thou shalt love thy neighbor as thyself.*", Leviticus 19:18

"*What is hateful to you, do not to your fellow man. This is the law: all the rest is commentary.*" Talmud, Shabbat 31a.

"*And what you hate, do not do to any one.*" Tobit 4:15 [4]

Native American Spirituality:

"*Respect for all life is the foundation.*" The Great Law of Peace.

"*All things are our relatives; what we do to everything, we do to ourselves. All is really One.*" Black Elk

"*Do not wrong or hate your neighbor. For it is not he who you wrong, but yourself.*" Pima proverb.

Roman Pagan Religion:

"The law imprinted on the hearts of all men is to love the members of society as themselves."

Shinto:

"The heart of the person before you is a mirror. See there your own form"

"Be charitable to all beings, love is the representative of God." Ko-ji-ki Hachiman Kasuga

Sikhism:

"Compassion-mercy and religion are the support of the entire world." Japji Sahib

"Don't create enmity with anyone as God is within everyone." Guru Arjan Devji 259

"No one is my enemy, none a stranger and everyone is my friend." Guru Arjan Dev : AG 1299

Sufism:

"The basis of Sufism is consideration of the hearts and feelings of others. If you haven't the will to gladden someone's heart, then at least beware lest you hurt someone's heart, for on our path, no sin exists but this." Dr. Javad Nurbakhsh, Master of the Nimatullahi Sufi Order.

Taoism:

"Regard your neighbor's gain as your own gain, and your neighbor's loss as your own loss." T'ai Shang Kan Ying P'ien.

"The sage has no interest of his own, but takes the interests of the people as his own. He is kind to the kind; he is also kind to the unkind: for Virtue is kind. He is faithful to the faithful; he is also faithful to the unfaithful: for Virtue is faithful." Tao Teh Ching, Chapter 49

Unitarian:

"We affirm and promote respect for the interdependent of all existence of which we are a part." Unitarian principles.

Yoruba (Nigeria):

"One going to take a pointed stick to pinch a baby bird should first try it on himself to feel how it hurts."

Zoroastrianism:

"That nature alone is good which refrains from doing unto another whatsoever is not good for itself". Dadistan-i-dinik 94:5

"Whatever is disagreeable to yourself do not do unto others." Shayast-na-Shayast 13:29

The roadmap of becoming who we should be has been part of our lives for thousands of years, and is as simple as four words; Do The Right Thing (DTRT). Our hearts and souls know what these actions are but we in so many cases refuse to listen.

The Golden Rule – is it new?

"What you would avoid suffering yourself, seek not to impose on others." (circa 100)

—Epictetus

"Act as if the maxim of thy action were to become by thy will a universal law of nature"

—Kant

"May I do to others as I would that they should do unto me." (Greece; 4th century)

—Plato

"Do not do to others that which would anger you if others did it to you." (Greece; 5th century)

—Socrates

"Treat your inferiors as you would be treated by your superiors." (Epistle 47:11 – Rome; 1st century)

—Seneca

Through our history and even in modern cinema we can see the Golden Rule and even the ripple effect – in the movie, "It's a Wonderful Life", we can see the ripple effect at its best, and how one person's life can be an ocean.

> *"Self-sacrifice is never entirely unselfish, for the giver never fails to receive."*
> —Dolores McGuire

1. *NationMaster.com* has an encyclopedia reference that lists many Golden Rules, sorted chronologically at: http://www.nationmaster.com/
2. *"Principles of Humanism,"* Humanist Association of Canada, at: http://canada.humanists.net/
3. This is Number 13 of a collection of 43 sayings of Prophet Muhammad (PBUH) that was compiled by the great Islamic scholar Yahya bin Sharaf Ul-Deen An-Nawawi. It is is now known as *"Al-Nawawi's Forty Hadiths"* See: http://www.dartmouth.edu/
4. The *Book of Tobit* is deuterocanonical, i.e. contained not in the Canon of Palestine but in that of Alexandria. It was accepted by some Jewish, Roman Catholic and Protestant traditions as part of the official canon but not by others.

"Strange, isn't it? Each man's life touches so many other lives. When he isn't around he leaves an awful hole, doesn't he?"
—Clarence from "It's a Wonderful Life"

Chapter 5

"It's a Wonderful Life"
What did George Bailey find out?

The summary in the 1946 movie, "It's A Wonderful Life", states "No one is born to be a failure. No one is poor who has friends." The movie exemplifies the ripple, the ocean, and the Golden Rule. The entire film is about being an ocean; let us look at one example from the movie.

The scene opens up to voices in the heaven's that are talking about a person in trouble (George Bailey – played by Jimmy Stewart), some of the voices are people praying for help; help for George Bailey. In answer to the pleads for help an angel (Clarence a humble watch maker who needs to get his wings) will be sent down to earth but first he had to know more about the young man in need, so opens the life history of George Bailey.

Clarence watches as George's story unfolds. We are only going to look at one example of George's life – we first see a young George playing on an iced over pond with a bunch of

Is Your Life a puddle or an Ocean

boys, yelling and having fun sliding along the ice. Then it is his young brother's turn to slide (Harry Bailey), but while Harry is sliding along the ice, he goes too far and breaks through a thin patch falling into the freezing water. George runs to the location where Harry fails through and dives in without thinking about his own safety. As a result of his actions he saves his brothers life but at a cost; he damages his ear due to the extreme cold.

During the movie, we can see several more examples of George's selflessness including spending his entire life giving of himself to the people of Bedford Falls. A little more background on the character of George Bailey – during his life George never became a famous architect or traveled like he dreamed but instead stayed in Bedford Falls (the town where the movie is based) helping people all around him. Now, Harry his brother went on to College and becomes a Navy pilot going on to save several men on a transport on D-day winning him the Congressional Medal of Honor while George stayed behind to keep the home fires burning and eventually run his fathers business.

Towards the end of the movie, George finds out that his company has misplaced a large sum of money that

> *"We shall never know all the good that a simple smile can do."*
> —Mother Teresa

cannot be accounted for which would result in bankruptcy and probably prison. After thinking about it he determines that with his life insurance policy, he is worth more dead than alive.

Now we see him on a bridge over an icy river jumping to his death – enter Clarence the angel. Who jumps into to the water first knowing that our hero George will save him. After pulling Clarence out of the water, George looks at him and says I cannot even kill myself right and wishes he would have never been born. His wish is granted.

George Bailey is now given a true gift, the ability to see how his life's journey had affected those around him (the ripples of his actions). Remember Harry, well George was never there to save him from breaking through the ice; Harry never went to college and never became a pilot and never saved the men on a military transport. Because George never existed he was not able to create the ripple of saving his brother – this absence resulted in thousands of people being effected. Think about each one of the men on the transport, they each had families or would have had families.

George realized that no matter how bad he thought his life had become it still was truly wonderful because of all the people he helped. Just like the ripple on the pond, his actions had far-reaching effects – who do you effect? After George realizes the truth about his life, he begs Clarence to return him to his life. George Bailey is an ocean.

The people we touch every day, our families, co-workers, and people we encounter in our community are part of us. We can go so far as to say that, we can influence people half way around the world by following the golden

> *"Everyday is a good day when you can wake up.*
> *Then you gauge each day on the intensity of how good they are."*
>
> —Richard Rowe

Is Your Life a puddle or an Ocean

rule. Every person we help here in our hometown will carry that action to those they meet and it will ripple forward...

I know what you are thinking, this is a movie not real life - true but real oceans exist and they have had the same impact as George.

"The best way to find yourself is to lose yourself in the service of others."

—Mohandas Gandhi

Chapter 6

Who are oceans past, present, positive and negative…

We saw an example of an ocean and the ripple effect in action. People create ripples just like the stone in a pond. We all have the ability to influence everyone we meet and these influences can be positive or negative. Our lives as oceans can likewise be positive or negative – think about the people around us, who has been a mentor or a hero that we want to emulate.

Here are some examples of Oceans both Positive and Negative:

Positive Oceans –

Mother Teresa
Mohandas Gandhi
Martin Luther King Jr.
Oprah Winfrey
Irena Sendler

Negative Oceans –

Adolf Hitler
Elizabeth Bathory
Elena Ceausescu
Benito Mosalini
Jim Jones

Remember that we see oceans in both ways. The ripples we create can be both positive and negative in nature so our lives become a result of how they influence. Most of the names we see here are familiar and the ripple they have created continues to resonate. One such person who affected others is Irena Sendler.

Irena was born in 1910 in the Warsaw suburb of Otwock. October 16, 1940 the German occupation ordered the construction of a wall to isolate the Warsaw Ghetto, relocating an estimated 450,000 Jewish citizens. The impossible conditions and lack of food resulted in deaths from starvation and disease, a plan to exterminate a race of people; adult and child alike. The ripple of evil was felt in varying ways across Warsaw but Irena had a different stone to throw.

In 1942, Irena became head of the Children's Department of the Council to Aid the Jews. She, among others created a secret underground and saved 2,500 children from certain death. During this time, the German troops were killing entire families, stamping out the history and future of a generation! Remember we talked about the pond and how we can see multiple ripples by several stones. Even some ripples can counter each other – Irena did just that.

Not only did Irena and her group save 2,500 children by smuggling them out of the ghetto in toolboxes, brick sacks and under truck seats; she maintained a record of each child's original Jewish name. Irena recorded every name and hid them in a jar, which she buried next to a tree across from a German barracks. Her underground group would then rename each child and give them to foster families that were not Jewish. After the war, she then reconnected all the original names with each child, saving the history of their family name. Even after being caught and tortured, Irena never divulged the location of the original names.

Irena created ripples that can be felt today; stop and think of the math – if 2,500 children grew up and got married, they then have 3 children of their own. Add three generations and we

2,500	saved
*	multiply
<u>3</u>	children born to each
7,500	total
*	multiply
<u>3</u>	generations
22,500	total as of 2003

can see that because of Irena and her group there is 22,500 people in this world making an impact, because of her group's actions. The amazing part of this story is that the ripple her group created continues today by each of the two thousand and five hundred children, generation after generation. Her ripple exceeded the pond limitations to become a wave of life throughout the world. In a recent interview by ABC, she was quoted as only doing what anyone else would have done.

One of the survivors, made a very powerful statement about what Irena and her group did – Elzbieta Ficowska was 6 months old when she was smuggled out of the ghetto in a pile of bricks, her parents died in the death camps, but she survived thanks to Sendler. "Irena represents the often forgotten <u>truth</u>, that no one should be indifferent."

> *"The world can be better if there's love, tolerance and humility."*
>
> —Irena Sendler

What is the difference between Irena and others? <u>Nothing</u>! It comes down to responsibility - in life's journey we need to help everyone along the path.

Part III

Being an ocean at
work, home & community

"Man must cease attributing his problems to his environment, and learn again to exercise his will – his personal responsibility."

—Albert Einstein

Chapter 7

Responsibility – who me...

Now comes the truth of our lives: "What responsibility do we assume for our actions, or even more powerful who is responsible?" In the previous chapter we looked at oceans and even gave an example of one person's life but most of all her ability to take responsibility, what does this word mean?

Responsibility – is a duty, <u>obligation,</u> or <u>burden</u>. We have an obligation or burden to initiate actions every day, every hour, every minute, and even every second that will effect us and those around us. When faced with responsibility do we look the other way and hope that someone else will take action to help others or do we embrace the chance to influence (create a positive ripple) in someone else's life?

> *"Knowing is not enough; we must apply. Willing is not enough; we must do."*
> —Johann Von Goethe

In life it is so easy to blame others for misfortunes. We are, to a degree responsible for everything that happens around us. Misfortune does happen but the responsibility, our part begins in our response to the misfortune. If Irena would have chosen a different responsibility and was only concerned for her own life, she would have been a puddle. Thousands of people may have ceased to exist. What if she had taken the path of least resistance, lived her life safe from harm, instead of "becoming" the resistance.

Today we have the same responsibility – every person we meet, or interact with needs our help. The help we are talking about may not be directly saving someone's life, it could be as simple as making him or her smile or just listening to them. Remember the ripple we have talked about, by "making someone's day" the ripple may carry to the next person they meet but it started with us.

Stop and think about how a simple action could change the outcome of someone else's behavior. What if we could stop abuse or suicide by acting upon our responsibilities? We are all intricately connected, whether or not we choose to accept our role of responsible for everything that happens around us. For example:

One Sunday I was attending church with my family, seated behind a young family with three small children. Half way through the service, we were supposed to shake hands and greet everyone around us. During the greeting, I watched a young father shake hands with the people around him, including his wife and the eldest daughter. Their middle child was laying on the pew right behind him. I observed that the two ½ year old reached a hand up to greet her father.

He was unaware of her actions, while their baby in her mother's arms reached out and shook the father's hand. The middle child's eyes watered and she continued to extend her hand. Feeling wronged, her chin quivered and she acted out her frustration for the next 10 minutes kicking and squirming in her seat. He concluded she was misbehaving and rebuked her actions during church. Was it the fathers fault for not trying to understand why his middle child was crying, or was it my responsibility to intervene or refrain from intruding on a family matter?

I may have stopped the whole event from going too far; just by tapping the young father on the shoulder and pointing out that, the little hand was reaching for him. (It makes my heart hurt thinking about that little chin as it quivered and knowing that I could have possibly changed the outcome of the event.) To amend the situation, I spoke with the father afterwards. Whether it changed prior events or the present moment, I'm not sure, but maybe a future misunderstanding might be avoided.

> "No alibi will save you from accepting the responsibility."
>
> —Napoleon Hill

If I had made the choice to accept my responsibility (obligation) to say something than it would have changed the outcome of the ripple that was created. There are always moments to amend and learn. What do we choose when faced with responsibility?

"I am responsible. Although I may not be able to prevent the worst from happening, I am responsible for my attitude toward the inevitable misfortunes that darken life. Bad things do

happen; how I respond to them defines my character and the quality of my life. I can choose to sit in perpetual sadness, immobilized by the gravity of my loss, or I can choose to rise from the pain and treasure the most precious gift I have – life itself."

—Walter Anderson

"You must choose the thoughts and actions that will lead you on to success."

—R. C. Allen

Chapter 8

Make a Choice…

What a powerful word – choice; the mental process of thinking involved with the process of judging the merits of multiple options and selecting one of them for action. Choices can be simple like getting out of bed, giving someone a smile, or complex, like saving someone's life, or giving a person the chance to improve their life.

Being a puddle or an ocean comes down to this; what do we choose to be! Why do people fail? They choose too; it is a

> *"There are two primary choices in life; to accept conditions as they exist, or accept the responsibility for changing them."*
>
> —Denis Waitley

harsh concept, but true. When we move through our journey in life, we will face hundreds of thousands of choices, for each one of these choices we create ripples that could be positive or negative. Every time we choose an action we can learn from the outcome, life is a cycle and we will have the chance to make an educated choice if the situation occurs again. Misfortunes occur natural or manmade and it is our choices that create the most favorable or unfavorable result.

Some of these choices come around repeatedly, like what we should have for dinner (we can determine what we like and do not like to eat); while other choices might only come around once or twice, whom we want to share our lives with or our career path.

To become an ocean we must face our choices that lead us to our responsibilities, and with choice, we can see how we influence those around us. We can measure our lives by many different theoretical models but when it comes down to it, we cannot depend on a doctor, co-worker, friend, or even family member to determine if we are a puddle or an ocean! We are the only ones that can determine what we are or what we will <u>become</u>.

> *"It's choice – not chance – that determines your destiny."*
> —Jean Nidetch

"We choose our joys and sorrows long before we experience them."

—Kahlil Gibran

"We are what we repeatedly do. Excellence, then, is not an act, but a habit."

—Aristotle

Chapter 9

The Tenants of becoming an ocean…

Even though we are the only ones that can answer the question, here are some possible guidelines to help us become the ocean that we want to be.

The Tenants of becoming an ocean

I. Acknowledging that you are solely responsible for the choices in your life.

II. Accepting that you are responsible for what you choose to feel or think.

III. Tearing down the mask of defense or rationale for why others are responsible for who you are.

IV. The rational belief that you are responsible for determining who you are, and how your choices affect your life and those around you.

V. Pointing the finger of responsibility back to <u>yourself</u> and away from others when you are discussing the consequences of your actions.

VI. Realizing that you determine your feelings, no matter how negative they seem.

VII. Recognizing that you are your best cheerleader; it is not reasonable or healthy for you to depend on others to make you feel good about yourself.

VIII. Letting go of your sense of over responsibility for others (everyone makes their own choices; all we can do is make the best choice possible and then allow the ripple to take control).

IX. Letting go of blame and anger toward those in your past who did the best they could, given the limitations of their knowledge, background, and awareness.

X. Understand why things happen, so that you can create success; not accept it as an accident.

BE EXTRAORDINARY IN YOUR LIFE BY POSITIVE ACTION

The Tenants of becoming an ocean...

What do you choose?
puddle or ocean

"Each day is a gift to be shared, provide value for others and you add value to yourself!"

—Richard Rowe

Woooooo Whooooo!!!

About the Author

Richard served over 20 years in the U. S. Navy achieving a certification for the military's Master Training Specialist (MTS) – this designation is awarded to only the top 10 percent of all military instructional staff, and is given to someone that demonstrates highly effective teaching/facilitation skills and a comprehensive knowledge of instructional design (ISD).

Richard has 15 years of experience in the training world, and brings that knowledge combined with passion to help people realize their true potential both in their professional and personal lives.

He is a member of ASTD, and the National Speakers Association (NSA). Richard is also the Chairman of CAV (a non-profit veteran's rights organization), appointed as an ESGR (Employer Support for Guard and Reserve) member by the DOD (Department of Defense); and holds an Associates degree in Technical Instruction, a Bachelors of Science in Business Administration with a focus on financial management and a Masters of Science in Management with a focus on adult learning.

www.jfgintl.com or e-mail oceans@jfgintl.com

Order Your Puddle or Ocean Training Curriculum Today.

Become an Ocean! Let Richard Rowe, internationally acclaimed author and speaker, further train you and your team on the tenants of being an ocean.

The Mission: To be an ocean at work, home, and in life. This curriculum is geared for relationships and even focuses on relationship sales – what do you choose to be?

Becoming an ocean:

1. **Ripple.** What ripples do you create?

2. **Responsibility.** Do you accept your responsibility?

3. **Choice.** What choices do you make?

4. **Tenants of an Ocean.** How do they apply to my life?

Visit www.jfgintl.com to order your curriculum.

Bring Richard Rowe to your organization!

Richard Rowe is known internationally as *"driven to excellence through passion."* His powerful presentations cover the topics of leadership, team building, customer service and mastering personal change. In addition to speaking, consulting, and training, allow Richard to share his passion and energy; it is contagious!

To Bring Richard Rowe to your organization go to www.jfgintl.com or e-mail oceans@jfgintl.com